**300 powerful quotes from top motivators
Tony Robbins Zig Ziglar Robert Kiyosaki
John Maxwell ... to lift you up.**

Copyright © 2014 – DOTCHAMOU ZAKARI

DEDICATION

This ebook is dedicated for you, you my wonderful readers who invest your valuable time, maybe your money in purchasing this ebook. I well know that without you, my dream of being a writer will be useless and unfulfilled.

Table of contents

INTRODUCTION

POWERFUL QUOTATIONS FROM ANTHONY ROBBINS

GREAT QUOTES FROM ZIG ZIGLAR

POWERFUL THOUGHTS FROM ROBERT KIYOSAKI

GREAT CITATIONS FROM JOHN C MAXWELL

OTHERS POWERFUL THOUGHTS FROM GREAT MINDS

INTRODUCTION

I don't know whether it is worth to be said, none of the ideas in this ebook comes from me. Most of these powerful quotes come from the best of the bests in the field of self help, self development and motivation. These brilliant masters are: Anthony Robbins, Zig Ziglar, Robert Kiyosaki, John Maxwell and other great thinkers.

What can a quote do for you? A quote is a powerful tool for our mind, our soul, our spirit. A quote can sharpen your

mind and give you an instant and rapid relief if your soul is down, in a dark time. A quote can guide you, can open your mind, and correct in a best way a wrong mindset, bad attitude, mediocrity... I don't have space in this ebook to tell you all the benefits a good quote can do for your life.

Now, how can you really benefit from this ebook?

Read it slowly. Take your time. Pause, that is why I make this ebook full of gaps and spaces, and ask yourself some questions like these: what is the lesson this quote is teaching me? Am I running my life with the principle in this quote? If I apply the principle in this quote, what will be the outcome in my life? What if I commit myself to applying on a daily basis the teaching of this quote?

If a particular quote strike your mind and mean something for you, please, take note, write it and put it in a place where your eyes will easily catch it. Maybe you will stick it in a wall ; you may put it into your pocket… Me, if a quote touches my heart, I even go on writing it in the palm of my hand, in my body… People think, I am mad. By doing that, I easily ingrain the meaning of the quote in my soul so that I can easily live my life by the teaching of the quote. If it good for you, you can try it.

Another way of gaining benefits from this ebook, is to read at least one or ten quotes every morning when you wake up and every night before sleeping. By doing that you will easily lift up your soul because, whether we want it or not, negativity is there, everywhere. We become sad and down without even noticing it, especially in the morning when we wake up. A good quote can quickly lift up a negative mind.

The fourth thing that you can do is to come back to this ebook if something goes wrong in your life. Maybe you can quickly find a quote that will help you to deal with the problem you have with more wisdom and positivity.

The last thing you have to do is to help at least one person by sharing this ebook with him. Like Jim Rhon said, everything we share helps us to grow and to have more.

Thank you very much, I wish for you all the best things, stay strong and full of wisdoms.

Powerful quotations from Tony Robbins

The secret of success is learning how to use pain and pleasure instead of having pain and pleasure use you. If you do that, you're in control of your life. If you don't, life controls you." – **Tony Robbins**

"I've come to believe that all my past failure and frustration were actually laying the foundation for the understandings that have created the new level of living I now enjoy." - **Tony Robbins**

"Identify your problems, but give your power and energy to solutions." - **Tony Robbins**

"Life is a gift, and it offers us the privilege, opportunity, and responsibility to give something back by becoming more." - **Tony Robbins**

"A real decision is measured by the fact that you've taken a new action. If there's no action, you haven't truly decided." – **Tony Robbins**

"New Year = A New Life! Decide today who you will

become, what you will give how you will live."
- *Tony Robbins*

"Leaders spend 5% of their time on the problem & 95% of their time on the solution. Get over it & crush it!"
- *Tony Robbins*

"One reason so few of us achieve what we truly want is that we never direct our focus; we never concentrate our power. Most people dabble their way through life, never deciding to master anything in particular." - *Tony Robbins*

"The only problem we really have is we think we're not supposed to have problems! Problems call us to higher level- – face & solve them now!" - *Tony Robbins*

"Your past does not equal your future." - *Tony Robbins*

"For changes to be of any true value, they've got to be lasting and consistent." - *Tony Robbins*

"I discovered a long time ago that if I helped enough people get what they wanted, I would always get what I wanted and I would never have to worry." - *Tony Robbins*

"Your life changes the moment you make a new, congruent, and committed decision." - *Tony Robbins*

"If you do what you've always done, you'll get what you've always gotten." - *Tony Robbins*

"It is in your moments of decision that your destiny is shaped." - *Tony Robbins*

"In life you need either inspiration or desperation."
- *Tony Robbins*

"Successful people ask better questions, and as a result, they get better answers." - *Tony Robbins*

"Things do not have meaning. We assign meaning to everything." - *Tony Robbins*

"Setting goals is the first step in turning the invisible into the visible." - *Tony Robbins*

"Only those who have learned the power of sincere and selfless contribution experience life's deepest joy: true fulfillment."
- *Tony Robbins*

"If you want to be successful, find someone who has achieved the results you want and copy what they do and you'll achieve the same results." - *Tony Robbins*

"I challenge you to make your life a masterpiece. I challenge you to join the ranks of those people who live what they teach, who walk their talk." - *Tony Robbins*

"It is not what we get. But who we become, what we contribute… that gives meaning to our lives."
- *Tony Robbins*

"People are not lazy. They simply have impotent goals – that is, goals that do not inspire them." - ***Tony Robbins***

"Beliefs have the power to create and the power to destroy. Human beings have the awesome ability to take any experience of their lives and create a meaning that disempowers them or one that can literally save their lives." - ***Tony Robbins***

Great quotes from Zig Ziglar

Remember there is plenty of room at the top

but not enough to sit down. Zig Ziglar

Selling is essentially a transference of feeling. Zig Ziglar

If you will pump long enough, hard enough,
and enthusiastically enough, sooner or later
the effort will bring forth the reward. Zig Ziglar

You don't "pay the price" for success
you enjoy the benefits of success. Zig Ziglar
Success is one thing you can't pay for. You buy it on the
installment plan and make payments every day. Zig Ziglar

Ability is important in our quest for success,
but dependability is critical. Zig Ziglar

Too many people spend more time planning how
to get the job than on how to become
productive and successful in that job. Zig Ziglar

You enhance your chances for success
when you understand that your yearning power
is more important than your earning power. Zig Ziglar

The price of success is much lower than the price of failure. Zig Ziglar

When management and labor (employer and employee)
both understand they are all on the same side,
then each will prosper more. Zig Ziglar

When we clearly understand that there is no superior sex
or superior race, we will have opened the door
of communication and laid the foundation
for building winning relationships with
all people in this global world of ours. Zig Ziglar

The only way to coast is down hill. Zig Ziglar

The greatest single cause of a poor self-image
is the absence of unconditional love. Zig Ziglar

It's not what you know, it's what you use
that makes a difference. Zig Ziglar

Success is not measured by what you do
compared to what others do, it is measured
by what you do with the ability God gave you. Zig Ziglar

Before you change your thinking,
you have to change what goes into your mind. Zig Ziglar

You are what you are and where you are because of
what has gone into your mind. You can change what you are and
where you are by changing what goes into your mind. Zig Ziglar

Don't be distracted by criticism. Remember,
the only taste of success some people have
is when they take a bite out of you. Zig Ziglar

If you don't like who you are and where you are, don't worry about it because you're not stuck either with who you are or where you are. You can grow. You can change. You can be more than you are. Zig Ziglar

Some people find fault like there is a reward for it. Zig Ziglar

Far too many people have no idea of what they can do because all they have been told is what they can't do. Zig Ziglar

They don't know what they want because
they don't know what's available for them. Zig Ziglar

Man was designed for accomplishment,
engineered for success, and endowed
with the seeds of greatness. Zig Ziglar

You were born to win, but to be the winner you were born to be you must plan to win and prepare to win. Then and only then can you legitimately expect to win.
Zig Ziglar

When your image improves, your performance improves.
Zig Ziglar

When I discipline myself to eat properly, live morally, exercise regularly, grow mentally and spiritually, and not put
any drugs or alcohol in my body, I have given myself the
freedom to be at my best, perform at my best,
and reap all the rewards that go along with it. Zig Ziglar

When we do more than we are paid to do,
eventually we will be paid more for what we do. Zig Ziglar

What comes out of your mouth

is determined by what goes into your mind. Zig Ziglar

You can get everything money will buy
without a lick of character, but you can't get
any of the things money won't buy—happiness,
joy, peace of mind, winning relationships, etc.,
without character. Zig Ziglar

What you do off the job is the determining factor
in how far you will go on the job. Zig Ziglar

You build a successful career, regardless of your
field of endeavor, by the dozens of little things
you do on and off the job. Zig Ziglar
When you exercise your freedom to express yourself
at the lowest level, you ultimately condemn
yourself to live at that level. Zig Ziglar

With integrity you have nothing to fear,
since you have nothing to hide. With integrity
you will do the right thing, so you will have no guilt.
With fear and guilt removed you are
free to be and do your best. Zig Ziglar

If standard of living is your major objective,
quality of life almost never improves, but if quality of life
is your number one objective, your standard of living
almost always improves. Zig Ziglar

If people like you they'll listen to you,
but if they trust you they'll do business with you. Zig Ziglar

Ability can take you to the top,
but it takes character to keep you there. Zig Ziglar

The quality of a person's life is in direct proportion
to his or her commitment to excellence,
regardless of his or her chosen field of endeavor. Zig Ziglar

Keep your thinking right and your business will be right. Zig Ziglar

When a company or an individual compromises one

time,
whether it's on price or principle,
the next compromise is right around the corner. Zig Ziglar

Our children are our only hope for the future,
but we are their only hope for their present and their future. Zig Ziglar

When you put faith, hope and love together
you can raise positive kids in a negative world. Zig Ziglar
 Failure is an event, not a person.
Yesterday ended last night. Zig Ziglar

There are seldom, if ever, any hopeless situations,
but there are many people who lose hope
in the face of some situations. Zig Ziglar

You cannot solve a problem until you acknowledge
that you have one and accept responsibility for solving it.

Zig Ziglar

Character gets you out of bed; commitment moves you
to action. Faith, hope, and discipline enable you
to follow through to completion. Zig Ziglar

The door to a balanced success opens widest
on the hinges of hope and encouragement. Zig Ziglar

I'm so optimistic I'd go after Moby Dick in a row boat
and take the tartar sauce with me. Zig Ziglar

Most of us would be upset if we were accused of being
"silly."
But the word "silly" comes from the old English word
"selig," and its literal definition is "to be
blessed, happy, healthy and prosperous." Zig Ziglar

The chief cause of failure and unhappiness is trading
what you want most for what you want now. Zig Ziglar

Be helpful. When you see a person without a smile, give him yours. Zig Ziglar

All of us perform better and more willingly when we know why we're doing what we have been told or asked to do. Zig Ziglar

Money will buy you a bed, but not a good night's sleep, a house but not a home, a companion but not a friend. Zig Ziglar

Most x-rated films are advertised as "adult entertainment,"
for "mature adults," when in reality they are juvenile entertainment for immature and insecure people.
Zig Ziglar

You don't drown by falling in water; you only drown if you stay there. Zig Ziglar
When you give a man a dole you deny him his dignity, and
when you deny him his dignity you rob him of his destiny.

Zig Ziglar

Remember, you can earn more money,
but when time is spent it is gone forever. Zig Ziglar

It's not the situation, but whether we react (negative)
or respond (positive) to the situation that's important.
Zig Ziglar

There's not a lot you can do about the national economy
but there is a lot you can do about your personal
economy.
Zig Ziglar

You can have everything in life you
want, if you will just help enough
other people get what they want. Zig Ziglar

Lack of direction, not lack of time, is the problem.
We all have twenty-four hour days. Zig Ziglar

You can finish school, and even make it easy –
but you never finish your education, and it is seldom

easy.
Zig Ziglar

The best way to make your spouse and children feel secure is not with big deposits in bank accounts, but with little deposits of thoughtfulness and affection in the "love account." Zig Ziglar

You've got to be before you can do,
and do before you can have. Zig Ziglar

If you're sincere, praise is effective.
If you're insincere, it's manipulative. Zig Ziglar

Everybody says they want to be free. Take the train off the tracks and it's free–but it can't go anywhere.
Zig Ziglar

Many marriages would be better if the husband and wife clearly understood that they're on the same side. Zig Ziglar

The more you express gratitude for what you have the more you will have to express gratitude for. Zig Ziglar

Kids go where there is excitement.
They stay where there is love. Zig Ziglar

Duty makes us do things well,
but love makes us do them beautifully. Zig Ziglar

When someone we love is having difficulty and is giving us a bad time, it's better to explore the cause than to criticize the action. Zig Ziglar

Take time to be quiet.
Obstacles are the things we see when we take our eyes off our goals. Zig Ziglar

The best thing a parent can do for a child

is to love his or her spouse. Zig Ziglar

Your mate doesn't live by bread alone; he or she needs to be "buttered up" from time to time. Zig Ziglar

Other people and things can stop you temporarily. You're the only one who can do it permanently. Zig Ziglar

Start your child's day with love and encouragement and end the day the same way. Zig Ziglar

You already have every characteristic necessary for success
if you recognize, claim, develop and use them. Zig Ziglar

You cannot make it as a wandering generality.
You must become a meaningful specific. Zig Ziglar

The best way to raise positive children in a negative world

is to have positive parents who love them unconditionally
and serve as excellent role models. Zig Ziglar

You will make a lousy anybody else,
but you will be the best "you" in existence. Zig Ziglar

You must manage yourself before you can
lead someone else. Zig Ziglar

Of all the "attitudes" we can acquire,
surely the attitude of gratitude is the most important
and by far the most life changing. Zig Ziglar

When you choose to be pleasant and positive in the
way you treat others, you have also chosen,
in most cases, how you are going to be treated by others.
Zig Ziglar

You can disagree without being disagreeable. Zig Ziglar

I've got to say no to the good so I can say yes to the best.
Zig Ziglar

To respond is positive, to react is negative. Zig Ziglar

Positive thinking will let you use the abilities,
training and experience you have. Zig Ziglar
 Positive thinking won't let you do anything but it will
let you do everything better than negative thinking will.
Zig Ziglar

We all need a daily check up from the neck up
to avoid stinkin' thinkin' which ultimately leads
to hardening of the attitudes. Zig Ziglar

It's not what happens to you that determines how far you
will go in life; it is how you handle what happens to you.
Zig Ziglar

You cannot tailor make the situations in life,
but you can tailor make the attitudes to
fit those situations before they arise. Zig Ziglar

What you get by reaching your destination is
not nearly as important as what you will become
by reaching your destination. Zig Ziglar

Motivation gets you going and habit gets you there.
Make motivation a habit and you will get there
more quickly and have more fun on the trip. Zig Ziglar

The basic goal-reaching principle is to understand
that you go as far as you can see, and when you
get there you will always be able to see farther. Zig Ziglar

You are the only one who can use your ability.
It is an awesome responsibility. Zig Ziglar

Your business is never really good or bad "out there."

Your business is either good or bad
right between your own two ears. Zig Ziglar

The real opportunity for success
lies within the person and not in the job. Zig Ziglar

It is easy to get to the top after you get
through the crowd at the bottom. Zig Ziglar

Success is not a destination, it's a journey.
The most practical, beautiful, workable philosophy
in the world won't work – if you won't. Zig Ziglar

Motivation is the fuel necessary
to keep the human engine running. Zig Ziglar
 Discipline yourself to do the things you need to do
when you need to do them, and the day will come
when you will be able to do the things you want to do
when you want to do them. Zig Ziglar

Ambition, fueled by compassion, wisdom and integrity, is a powerful force for good that will turn the wheels of industry and open the doors of opportunity for you and countless others. Zig Ziglar

If we don't start, it's certain we can't arrive. Zig Ziglar

Obviously, there is little you can learn from doing nothing.
Zig Ziglar

Powerful thoughts from Robert Kiyosaki

"The trouble with school is they give you the answer, then they give you the exam. That's not life." - **Robert Kiyosaki**

"Complaining about your current position in life is worthless. Have a spine and do something about it instead." - **Robert Kiyosaki**

"The fear of being different prevents most people from

seeking new ways to solve their problems." - **Robert Kiyosaki**

"Winners are not afraid of losing. But losers are. Failure is part of the process of success. People who avoid failure also avoid success." - **Robert Kiyosaki**

"Successful people ask questions. They seek new teachers. They're always learning." - **Robert Kiyosaki**

"If you want to be rich, you need to develop your vision. You must be standing on the edge of time gazing into the future." - **Robert Kiyosaki**

"If you're still doing what mommy and daddy said for you to do (go to school, get a job, and save money), you're losing." - **Robert Kiyosaki**

"Often, the more money you make the more money you spend; that's why more money doesn't make you rich – assets make you rich." - **Robert Kiyosaki**

"The most life destroying word of all is the word

tomorrow." - **Robert Kiyosaki**

"The size of your success is measured by the strength of your desire; the size of your dream; and how you handle disappointment along the way." - **Robert Kiyosaki**

"I'd rather welcome change than cling to the past." - **Robert Kiyosaki**

"The most successful people are mavericks who aren't afraid to ask why, especially when everyone thinks it's obvious." - **Robert Kiyosaki**

"Hoping drains your energy. Action creates energy." - **Robert Kiyosaki**

"The more a person seeks security, the more that person gives up control over his life." - **Robert Kiyosaki**

"Everyone can tell you the risk. An entrepreneur can see the reward." - **Robert Kiyosaki**

"A plan is a bridge to your dreams. Your job is to make the plan or bridge real, so that your dreams will become real. If all you do is stand on the side of the bank and dream of the other side, your dreams will forever be just dreams. - **Robert Kiyosaki**

"You'll often find that it's not mom or dad, husband or wife, or the kids that's stopping you. It's you. Get out of your own way." - **Robert Kiyosaki**

"The only difference between a rich person and poor person is how they use their time" - **Robert Kiyosaki**
 "Your choices decide your fate. Take the time to make the right ones. If you make a mistake, that's fine; learn from it & don't make it again." - **Robert Kiyosaki**

"If you're the kind of person who has no guts, you just give up every time life pushes you. If you're that kind of person, you'll live all your life playing it safe, doing the right things, saving yourself for something that never happens. Then, you die a boring old person." - **Robert Kiyosaki**

"Money is really just an idea." - **Robert Kiyosaki**

"Talk is cheap. Learn to listen with your eyes. Actions do speak louder than words. Watch what a person does more than what he says." - **Robert Kiyosaki**

"The moment you make passive income and portfolio income a part of your life, your life will change. Those words will become flesh." - **Robert Kiyosaki**

"You will make some mistakes but, if you learn from those mistakes, those mistakes will become wisdom and wisdom is essential to becoming wealthy." - **Robert Kiyosaki**

"If you realize that you're the problem, then you can change yourself, learn something and grow wiser. Don't blame other people for your problems." - **Robert Kiyosaki**

"Workers work hard enough to not be fired, and owners pay just enough so that workers won't quit." - **Robert Kiyosaki**

"As I said, I wish I could say it was easy. It wasn't, but it wasn't hard either. But without a strong reason or purpose, anything in life is hard. " - **Robert Kiyosaki**

"The single most powerful asset we all have is our mind. If it is trained well, it can create enormous wealth in what seems to be an instant." - **Robert Kiyosaki**

"Find the game where you can win, and then commit your life to playing it; and play to win." - **Robert Kiyosaki**

"The power of "can't": The word "can't" makes strong people weak, blinds people who can see, saddens happy people, turns brave people into cowards, robs a genius of their brilliance, causes rich people to think poorly, and limits the achievements of that great person living inside us all." - **Robert Kiyosaki**

"One of the great things about being willing to try new things and make mistakes is that making mistakes keeps you humble. People who are humble learn more than people who are arrogant." - **Robert Kiyosaki**

"Intelligence solves problems and produces money. Money without financial intelligence is money soon gone." - **Robert Kiyosaki**

"Start small and dream big." - **Robert Kiyosaki**

"Emotions are what make us human. Make us real. The word 'emotion' stands for energy in motion. Be truthful about your emotions, and use your mind and emotions in your favor, not against yourself." – **Robert Kiyosaki**

"You're only poor if you give up. The most important thing is that you did something. Most people only talk and dream of getting rich. You've done something." - **Robert Kiyosaki**

"If you want to be financially-free, you need to become a different person than you are today and let go of whatever has held you back in the past." - **Robert Kiyosaki**

"The philosophy of the rich and the poor is this: the rich invest their money and spend what is left. The poor spend their money and invest what is left." - **Robert Kiyosaki**

"Sight is what you see with your eyes, vision is what you see with your mind." - **Robert Kiyosaki**

"In school we learn that mistakes are bad, and we are punished for making them. Yet, if you look at the way humans are designed to learn, we learn by making mistakes. We learn to walk by falling down. If we never fell down, we would never walk." - **Robert Kiyosaki**

"Never say you cannot afford something. That is a poor man's attitude. Ask HOW to afford it." - **Robert Kiyosaki**

"F.O.C.U.S – Follow One Course Until Successful" -

Robert Kiyosaki

"Your future is created by what you do today, not tomorrow" - **Robert Kiyosaki**

"I find so many people struggling, often working harder, simply because they cling to old ideas. They want things to be the way they were; they resist change. Old ideas are their biggest liability. It is a liability simply because they fail to realize that while that idea or way of doing something was an asset yesterday, yesterday is gone."
- **Robert Kiyosaki**

"The more I risk being rejected, the better my chances are of being accepted." - **Robert Kiyosaki**

"One of the most stupid things to do is to pretend you are smart. When you pretend to be smart, you are at the height of stupidity."
- **Robert Kiyosaki**

"Find out where you are at, where you are going and build a plan to get there." - **Robert Kiyosaki**

"I am concerned that too many people are focused too much on money and not on their greatest wealth, which is their education. If people are prepared to be flexible, keep an open mind and learn, they will grow richer and richer through the changes. If they think money will solve the problems, I am afraid those people will have a rough ride."
- **Robert Kiyosaki**

"Most people want everyone else in the world to change themselves. Let me tell you, it's easier to change yourself than everyone else." - **Robert Kiyosaki**

"People who dream small dreams continue to live as small people." - **Robert Kiyosaki**
"The richest people in the world build networks; everyone else is trained to look for work." - **Robert Kiyosaki**

"There are those who make things happen, there are those who watch things happen and there are those who say 'what happened?" - **Robert Kiyosaki**

"Skills make you rich, not theories." - **Robert Kiyosaki**

"Losers quit when they fail. Winners fail until they succeed."
- **Robert Kiyosaki**

"When you come to the boundaries of what you know, it is time to make some mistakes." - **Robert Kiyosaki**

"People without financial knowledge, who take advice from financial experts are like lemmings simply following their leader. They race for the cliff and leap into the ocean of financial uncertainty, hoping to swim to the other side." - **Robert Kiyosaki**

"The ability to sell is the number one skill in business. If you cannot sell, don't bother thinking about becoming a business owner."
- **Robert Kiyosaki**

"Too many people are too lazy to think. Instead of

learning something new, they think the same thought day in day out." - **Robert Kiyosaki**

"Education is cheap; experience is expensive." - **Robert Kiyosaki**

"There are no mistakes in life, just learning opportunities."
- **Robert Kiyosaki**

"The love of money is not the root of all evil. The lack of money is the root of all evil." - **Robert Kiyosaki**

"We all have tremendous potential, and we all are blessed with gifts. Yet, the one thing that holds all of us back is some degree of self-doubt. It is not so much the lack of technical information that holds us back, but more the lack of self-confidence." - **Robert Kiyosaki**

"When you are forced to think, you expand your mental capacity. When you expand your mental capacity, your

wealth increases."
- **Robert Kiyosaki**

"Making mistakes isn't enough to become great. You must also admit the mistake, and then learn how to turn that mistake into an advantage." - **Robert Kiyosaki**

"In today's rapidly changing world, the people who are not taking risk are the risk takers." - **Robert Kiyosaki**

"Tomorrows only exist in the minds of dreamers and losers"
- **Robert Kiyosaki**

"Excuses cost a dime and that's why the poor could afford a lot of it." - **Robert Kiyosaki**

People need to wake up and realize that life doesn't wait for you. If you want something, get up and go after it." -
 Robert Kiyosaki

"If you want to be rich, simply serve more people." - **Robert Kiyosaki**

"You're only poor if you give up. The most important thing is that you did something. Most people only talk and dream of getting rich. You've done something." - **Robert Kiyosaki**

"When people are lame, they love to blame." - **Robert Kiyosaki**

"Inside each of us is a David and a Goliath." - **Robert Kiyosaki**

"It is easy to stay the same but it is not easy to change. Most people choose to stay the same all their lives." - **Robert Kiyosaki**

"It does not take money to make money." - **Robert Kiyosaki**

"Face your fears and doubts, and new worlds will open

to you."
- **Robert Kiyosaki**

"A mistake is a signal that it is time to learn something new, something you didn't know before." - **Robert Kiyosaki**

"There are no bad business and investment opportunities, but there are bad entrepreneur and investors." - **Robert Kiyosaki**

"A winning strategy must include losing." - **Robert Kiyosaki**

"If you want to go somewhere, it is best to find someone who has already
been there." - **Robert Kiyosaki**

"Success is a poor teacher. We learn the most about ourselves when we fail, so don't be afraid of failing. Failing is part of the process of success. You cannot have success without failure." - **Robert Kiyosaki**

"The wealthy buy luxuries last, while the poor and middle-class tend to buy luxuries first. Why? Emotional discipline." - **Robert Kiyosaki**
 To be a successful business owner and investor, you have to be emotionally neutral to winning and losing. Winning and losing are just part of the game." - **Robert Kiyosaki**

"The problem with having a job is that it gets in the way of getting rich." - **Robert Kiyosaki**

"When times are bad is when the real entrepreneurs emerge."
- **Robert Kiyosaki**

"Sometimes you win, sometimes you learn." - **Robert Kiyosaki**

"You get one life. Live it in a way that it inspires

someone."
- **Robert Kiyosaki**

"The biggest challenge you have is to challenge your own self doubt and your laziness. It is your self doubt and your laziness that defines and limit who you are." - **Robert Kiyosaki**

"When I started my last business, I didn't receive a paycheck for 13 months. The average person can't handle that pressure."
- **Robert Kiyosaki**

"Getting rich begins with the right mindset, the right words and the right plan." - **Robert Kiyosaki**

"Sometimes, what is right for you at the beginning of your life is not the right thing for you at the end of your life." - **Robert Kiyosaki**

"Business is like a wheel barrow. Nothing happens until you start pushing." - **Robert Kiyosaki**
Starting a business is like jumping out of an airplane

without a parachute. In mid air, the entrepreneur begins building a parachute and hopes it opens before hitting the ground." - **Robert Kiyosaki**

"Business and investing are team sports." - **Robert Kiyosaki**

"If you want to be rich the rule of thumb is to teach others how to be rich." – **Robert Kiyosaki**

"The hardest part of change is going through the unknown."
- **Robert Kiyosaki**

"Financial struggle is often the direct result of people working all their lives for someone else." - **Robert Kiyosaki**

"Being an entrepreneur is simply going from one mistake to the next. You must have the fortitude to continue on." - **RobertKiyosaki**

Great quotes from John c Maxwell

"If you start today to do the right thing, you are already a success even if it doesn't show yet." - *John Maxwell*

"Change is inevitable. Growth is optional." – *John Maxwell*

"The greatest mistake we make is living in constant fear that we will make one." - *John Maxwell*

"Leadership is not about titles, positions or flowcharts. It is about one life influencing another." - *John Maxwell*

"Doing the right thing daily, compounds over time." - *John Maxwell*

"If we are growing we are always going to be outside

our comfort zone." - **John Maxwell**

"The pessimist complains about the wind. The optimist expects it to change. The leader adjusts the sails." - **John Maxwell**

"Life is 10% of what happens to me and 90% of how I react to it." - **John Maxwell**

"Talent is a gift, but character is a choice." - **John Maxwell**

"Learn to say 'no' to the good so you can say 'yes' to the best." - **John Maxwell**

"We cannot become what we need by remaining what we are." - **John Maxwell**

"Failing forward" is the ability to get back up after you've been knocked down, learn from your mistake, and move forward in a better direction." - **John Maxwell**

"Success is…knowing your purpose in life, growing to reach your maximum potential, and sowing seeds that benefit others." - ***John Maxwell***

"The more seriously you take your growth, the more seriously your people will take you." - ***John Maxwell***

"Most People have a desire to look for the exception instead of the desire to become exceptional." - ***John Maxwell***

"Speak the truth. Transparency breeds legitimacy." - ***John Maxwell***

"Make a point to continually search for a better way of doing things, even when things are going well, to ensure that a better alternative has not been overlooked and to keep your creative talents in practice." - ***John Maxwell***

"Creative leaders inherently know when rules need to be challenged, and they can see when a more flexible

approach should be taken." - *John Maxwell*
"Although it's admirable to be ambitious and hard-working, it's more desirable to be smart-working." - *John Maxwell*

"The timing of your decision is just as important as the decision you make." - *John Maxwell*

"A great leader's courage to fulfill his vision comes from passion, not position." - *John Maxwell*

"A man must be big enough to admit his mistakes, smart enough to profit from them, and strong enough to correct them." - *John Maxwell*
"Happiness simply cannot be relied upon as a measure of success." - *John Maxwell*

"Often people fail to start or complete a task because they don't see any connection between what they're doing andwhat they really want to accomplish in life." - *John Maxwell*

"You cannot overestimate the unimportance of practically everything." - *John Maxwell*

"Leaders don't rise to the pinnacle of success without developing the right set of attitudes and habits; they make every day a masterpiece." - *John Maxwell*

"Reaching the top is a monumental achievement, but remaining there may be the most spectacular feat of all." - *John Maxwell*

"You build trust with others each time you choose integrity over image, truth over convenience, or honor over personal gain." - *John Maxwell*

"Earn the right to be heard by listening to others. Seek to understand a situation before making judgments about it." - *John Maxwell*

"Leaders never outgrow the need to change." - ***John Maxwell***

"If you don't have peace, it isn't because someone took it from you; you gave it away. You cannot always control what happens to you, but you can control what happens in you." - ***John Maxwell***

"Plan and execute your first failure so that you no longer have to fear it." - ***John Maxwell***

"The only guarantee for failure is to stop trying" - ***John Maxwell***

"The greatest day in your life and mine is when we take total responsibility for our attitudes. That's the day we truly grow up." - ***John Maxwell***

"Stay focused instead of getting offended or off track by others." - ***John Maxwell***

"To add value to others, one must first value others." - *John Maxwell*

"Doing the wrong thing daily, compounds over time." - *John Maxwell*

"There are two paths people can take. They can either play now and pay later, or pay now and play later. Regardless of the choice, one thing is certain. Life will demand a payment." - *John Maxwell*

"The difference between average people and achieving people is their perception of and response to failure." - *John Maxwell*

"As you begin changing your thinking, start immediately to change your behavior. Begin to act the part of the person you would like to become. Take action on your behavior. Too many people want to feel, then take action. This never works." - *John Maxwell*

"It's true that charisma can make a person stand out for a moment, but character sets a person apart for a lifetime." - *John Maxwell*

"Everything begins with a decision. Then, we have to manage that decision for the rest of your life." - *John Maxwell*

"If you don't change the direction you are going, then you're likely to end up where you're heading…" - *John Maxwell*

"People may hear your words, but they feel your attitude." - *John Maxwell*

"The unsuccessful person is burdened by learning, and prefers to walk down familiar paths. Their distaste for learning stunts their growth and limits their influence." - *John Maxwell*

"Success is due to our stretching to the challenges of life. Failure comes when we shrink from them." - *John Maxwell*

Others powerful citations from great minds

"Today I will do what others won't, so tomorrow I can accomplish what others can't."
Jerry Rice

"Losers quit when they're tired. Winners quit when they've won."
Unknown

"To get something you never had, you have to do something you've never done."
Unknown

"Some people dream of success… others stay awake to achieve it."
Unknown

"You miss 100 percent of the shots you don't take"
Wayne Gretzky

"Your time is limited, so don't waste it living someone else's life."
Steve Jobs

"Some people want it to happen, some wish it would happen, others make it happen." Michael Jordan

"It took us so long to realize that a purpose of human life, no matter who is controlling it, is to love whoever is around to be loved."
Kurt Vonnegut

"There are only two ways to live your life. One is as though nothing is a miracle. The other is as though everything is a miracle."
Albert Einstein

"You may be disappointed if you fail, but you are doomed if you don't try."
Beverly Sills

"Do what you can with what you've got wherever you are."
Theodore Roosevelt

"Use what talents you possess; the woods would be very silent if no birds sang except those that sang best."
Henry Van Dyke

"It is not length of Life, but depth of life."
Ralph Waldo Emerson

"We all take different paths in life, but no matter where we go, we take a little of each other everywhere."
Tim McGraw

"Laughter is the music of life."
Sir William Osler

"In the province of the mind, what one believes to be true either is true or becomes true."
John Lilly

"Experience is the hardest kind of teacher. It gives you the test first and the lesson afterward."
Author Unknown

"Friendship makes prosperity more shining and lessens adversity by dividing and sharing it."
Cicero, 44 B.C.

"In the giving-is the getting."
David Matoc

"The impossible is often the untried."
Jim Goodwin

"Anyone can become angry-that is easy, but to become angry with the right person, to the right degree, at the right time, for the right purpose, and in the right way-that is not easy."
Aristotle

"Character, in great and little things, means carrying through what you feel able to do."
Goethe, 1749-1832

"Don't let yesterday use up too much of today."
Will Rogers

"My religion is very simple, my religion is kindness."
Dalai Lama

"The important thing is to not stop questioning."
Albert Einstein, 1879-1955

"It's not your circumstances that shape you, it's how you react to your circumstances."
Anne Ortlund

"The best thing about the future is that it only comes one day at a time."
Abraham Lincoln

"Peace comes from within. Do not seek it without."
Buddha

"It takes strength to be gentle and kind."
Stephen Morrisey

"A hero is a person who does what he or she can."
Roman Rolland

"What lies behind us and what lies before us are small matter compared to what lies within us."

Ralph Waldo Emerson

"Where there is unity there is always victory."
PubliliusSyrus

"The greatest mistake you can make in life is to be continually fearing you will make one."
E. Hubbard

"The only thing standing between you and your goal is the bullshit story you keep telling yourself as to why you can't achieve it."
Jordan Belfort

"Never regret. If it's good, it's wonderful. If it's bad, it's experience." ***Victoria Holt***

"It's not denial. I'm selective about the reality I accept."
Calvin

"The great thing about getting older is that you don't lose all the other ages you've been."
Madeleine L'Engle

"We ourselves feel that what we are doing is just a drop in the ocean. But the ocean would be less because of that missing drop."
Mother Teresa

"I like nonsense,it wakens up the brain cells. Fantasy is a necessary ingredient in living, it's a way of looking at life through the wrong end of a telescope and that enables you to laugh at life's realities."
Dr. Seuss

"A positive attitude may not solve all your problems, but it will annoy enough people to make it worth the effort."
Herm Albright

"Nothing is worth more than this day."
Goethe

"Never doubt that a small group of thoughtful citizens can change the world. Indeed, it is the only thing that ever has."
Margaret Mead

"If at first you don't succeed, you're running about average."
M.H. Alderson

"Life is like a ten speed bike. Most of us have gears we never use."
Charles Schultz

"There is nothing permanent except change."
Heraditus

"The miracle is this; the more we share, the more we have."
Leonard Nimoy

"Out of clutter, find simplicity; from discord, find harmony; in the middle of difficulty, lies opportunity."
Albert Einstein

"Hope is like a road in the country. There never was a road; but, when many people walk together, the road comes into existence."

From the National Organization for Rare Disorders, Inc.

"Never give up on a dream just because of the time it will take to accomplish it. Especially when that time will pass you by anyway."
Unknown

"Dreams come true; without that possibility, nature would not incite us to have them."
John Updike, 1989, U.S. author & critic

"Our greatest glory is not failing, but in rising every time we fail."
Confucius

"Be more concerned with your character than your reputation, because your character is what you really are, while your reputation is merely what others think you are."
John Wooden

"Happiness is inward, and not outward; and so, it does not depend on what we have, but on what we are."
Henry Van Dyke

"A wise man should have money in his head, but not in

his heart."
Jonathan Swift

"The pain you feel today is the strength you feel tomorrow."
Unknown

"Worry is as useless as a handle on a snowball."
Mitzi Chandler

"The strongest oak of the forest is not the one that is protected from the storm and hidden from the sun. It's the one that stands in the open where it is compelled to struggle for its existence against the wind and rains and the scorching sun."
Napoleon Hill

"It's not the load that breaks you down; it's the way you carry it."
Lena Horne

"Keep you face to the sunshine and you cannot see the shadow."
Helen Keller

"If you don't go after what you want, you'll never have it. If you don't ask, the answer is always no. If you don't step foward your always in the same place."
Nora Roberts

"A good hand and a good heart are always a formidable combination."
Nelson Mandela

"There are two ways of exerting ones strength; one is pushing down, the other is pulling up."
Booker T. Washington

"A person that values it's privileges above its principles soon loses both."
Dwight Eisenhower

"It is difficult to say what is impossible, for the dream of yesterday is the hope of today and the reality of tomorrow."
Robert H. Goddard

"Never deprive someone of hope; it may be all they have."
H. Jackson Brown Jr.

"We make a living by what we get; we make a life by what we give."
Sir Winston Churchill

"It is better to look ahead and prepare than to look back and regret"
Jackie Joyner-Kersee

"We all have a few failures under our belt. It's what makes us ready for the successes."
Randy K. Milholland

 "Don't count every hour in the day, make every hour in the day count."
Anonymous
"If you want others to be happy, practice compassion. If you want to be happy, practice compassion."
The Dalai Lama

"Learn from yesterday, live for today, hope for tomorrow."
Albert Einstein

"The faintest ink is better than the best memory"
Unknown

. "Every dog must have his day."
Jonathan Swift
"Dear tomorrow, do whatever you want to do. I have already lived my today and I am not afraid of you

anymore.''
Unknown

"Successful people are simply those with successful habits."
 - **Brian Tracy**

"The ability to discipline yourself to delay gratification in the short term in order to enjoy greater rewards in the long term, is the indispensable prerequisite for success." - **Brian Tracy**

"You have within you right now, everything you need to deal with whatever the world can throw at you." - **Brian Tracy**

CPSIA information can be obtained
at www.ICGtesting.com
Printed in the USA
BVHW071458260620
582152BV00003B/395